Unveiled

Unveiled

Published 2025 by Sandra Behan
Copyright © Sandra Behan
ISBN: 978-1-916544-80-2

All rights reserved. No part of this publication may be reproduced or transmitted in any form or by any means, electronic or mechanical, including photography, recording, or any information storage or retrieval system without permission in writing from Sandra Behan. The book is sold subject to the condition that it shall not, by way of trade or otherwise, be lent, copied, altered, resold or otherwise circulated without Sandra Behan's prior consent.

Publishing Information

Design & publishing services provided by JM Agency

www.jm.agency
Kerry, Ireland

Unveiled

A Collection of Poetry

Sandra Behan

Dedication

To my daughters, Jennifer, Anne-Marie, and Paula—this book is my legacy to you.

To my grandchildren Darragh, Kayla and Aaron. Aaron calls me "Nanny the writer" and co-wrote 'Boy Racer' with me.

To my partner, TJ, for your unwavering support and careful edits.

To my friend Aoife, for your curiosity, research, and support.

To my colleague Ian, for constantly pushing me to keep going.

To Neil, for your wonderful cover photo that captures the spirit of this book.

To the community of Listowel, for encouraging and believing in me to share my voice and pursue my dream of becoming a writer.

To Jeremy, Parvathi, Kezia and the team at JM Agency for the unwavering support and encouragement.

And finally, to all those—family, friends, and well-wishers—who offered their encouragement, kindness, and support along the way. This book carries a piece of each of you.

CONTENTS

PART ONE

Dancing with the Daffodils	13
Wildflowers in the April Rain	15
Magnificent Red Kite	16
Trá Mór Beach	18
Sunrise by the Boardwalk – A Healing Moment	20
The Silent Dawn	22
A Tranquil Lunch by the Canal	24
Buddy	26
Gooseberries	28
Moyteoge Head	29
In the Still of Night	32
Aunty May	34
She Says	36
Corned Beef and Cabbage	38
Sunrise	40
Saint Brigid's Day	41

PART TWO

First Love	45
My Guiding Light	47
Is it a Lie?	49

Why Did You Not Call?	50
Between Us	52
In the Stillness of This Hour	54
An Unanchored Reality	56
The Ageless Warrior	58
Christmas Eve	60
A Christmas Prayer	61
Mother's Day 2022	63
Baking with My Mother	65
The Dance	68
Framed by Grief	70
The Ravages of War	72
Tides of Emotion	75

PART THREE

Shadows in the Dusk	79
Manipulation of the Heart	81
The Unveiled Woman	82
Butterfly	83
Bumblebee	85
I Never Left	87
Childhood Memories	89
Echoes of Baravore – The Old Crusher House	91
A Miners' Week Beneath Glass Mountain's Veil	94

Edenderry – Echoes of a Bygone Era	97
Seamus Heaney – A Decade's Tribute	100
Year's End to New Beginnings	101
Hope and Greed	103
Ripples of Time	104
Justice	106

PART FOUR

Boy Racer	111
Ballad of McGrath's Army	113
Macken Street	115
Captured in a Digital Age	117
The Road Between Us	118
Photographer's Journey at Serenity's Cove	120
The Bridge	123
Benbulben	125
Nollaig na mBan	127
Bloomsday	129
Twelve Crosses at Ballybraid	131
In the Darkness of the Night	133
Trapped in an Hourglass	134
About the Author	136

PART ONE

PART ONE

Dancing with the Daffodils

In the gentle light of spring,
I wander through fields,
alone but at peace,
where the earth breathes softly
and the grass whispers beneath my feet.

Here, I find a cluster of daffodils—
golden heads bobbing like cheerful suns,
bright against the soft green,
each petal a reminder of joy,
of days when the world felt simple
and full of wonder.

They sway in the warm breeze,
whispering secrets
like laughter echoing in the stillness.
I sit beside them,
wrapped in their sweet fragrance,
lost in this moment of beauty,
where time pauses
and the burdens of life fall away.

I linger here,
surrounded by colour and life,
my spirit lifted,
my heart made lighter
in this sacred space
where nature sings,
and I am reminded
of the quiet joys
that dance in the open fields.

Wildflowers in the April Rain

In April rain, I stand and wait,
For marmalade horizons to abate,
The russet ruffles of azure spring,
And the colourless canvas clouds they bring.

The rain falls softly on my skin,
And I feel something stir within—
A longing for the beauty I see
In the flowers, the clouds, and the sea.

I want to capture it all, to hold it tight,
To make it mine, to bring it to light.
I know it's not mine to claim.
It's a gift of nature, a living flame.

So, I stand and watch, and let it be—
The wildflowers, the rain, and the sea.
And I know that even as I strive,
The beauty of this world will always survive.

Magnificent Red Kite

I step out of my everyday world
and find a quiet peace within.
Going deep into nature,
surrounded by familiar trees.

The beauty of purple heather,
the inspiration of mountains,
the warmth of the sun.
I feel tranquillity's gentle embrace,
enter my body, mind, and spirit.

I see a rising shadow,
I hear a shrill, mewing 'peee-ooow'.
In flight, the Red Kite so serene,
seldom heard and rarely seen—
a silent glide, mute in nature.

Soaring on long wings,
its forked tail twisting
as it changes direction,
evaluating flits by length and breadth,
eyeing with a piercing gaze.

Scavengers drifting below,
searching for food on the ground.
Wary, it waits until it's safe to land,
with a distinctive walk, stealthy,
without making a sound.

In a high deciduous tree,
where such elegance makes nest—
joy when out walking,
a gift for me—
the Red Kite gliding silently.

Trá Mór Beach

In Donegal, where land meets sea,
I stand at the world's edge.
The shoreline stretches like a promise;
Soft sands beneath my bare feet—
Each grain a memory of past times.

Mountains rise, rugged and strong;
Muckish* watches from afar.
The air, rich with salt and peat,
Carries old stories in the wind.

Waves crash, steady and rhythmic,
Singing songs of freedom.
I breathe the sharp, briny air,
Feel the sun's warmth,
Reminded that I belong here.

Meadow blooms unfurl in bright colours—
Reds, yellows and purples against green.
Their sweet scent mingles with earth;
Each petal a burst of life,
Each breeze a call to be.

Time lingers on the boardwalk;
Foam curls at my side.
Thoughts rise and fade with the tide.
The wind whispers: remember, create, dream.
In Donegal, beauty is felt—
A quiet awakening stirs my soul.
In this vastness, I am small yet significant,
Held by nature, where worries dissolve like dawn mist.

---

*A mountain in the Derryveagh Mountains in County Donegal, Ireland.

Sunrise by the Boardwalk – A Healing Moment

In the stillness before dawn,
I walk the boardwalk,
where ocean kisses land.
The salty breeze whispers against my face,
waves sing their familiar song.

Rain falls softly—each drop a gentle reminder,
inviting me to pause,
to breathe,
to feel.

With tea in hand—lemon, honey, ginger—
warm against the chill,
I stand still, letting the world unfold.
Seagulls circle above,
their calls echoing in the morning light.
I soak in the beauty of this new day.

I notice remnants of sandcastles—
tiny fortresses left behind,
a child's abandoned sunglasses.
Small details, reminders of joy
and laughter from yesterday.

The sunrise breaks—a promise of fresh starts,
an invitation to let go,
to begin again,
with friends by my side,
accepting each moment with an open heart.

In this quiet space, I find calm,
a chance to simply be,
to feel grateful for the beauty around me.
As the sun rises higher,
filling the sky with light,
I am here—alive, thankful.

The Silent Dawn

I sit in complete darkness by the window,
Patiently waiting for the sunrise.
Before me, Doughbeg Beach in Mulranny,
Veiled in obsidian—
A tranquil haven in the quiet of October.

The grazing sheep and goats,
Mere silhouettes against the inky night.
As the world outside transitions
From black to a soft, dark blue,
A sense of anticipation stirs within me.

I can feel the slow, gradual shift,
The earth waking from its slumber,
The horizon whispering secrets of light.
In this hush, I find a kind of magic—
A promise that each day brings
new beginnings.

The stillness wraps around me
Like a warm blanket,
And I breathe in the quiet,
Relishing the moments before dawn breaks,
When everything feels possible,

And the world holds its breath,
Awaiting the sun's gentle embrace.

With each passing second,
The darkness begins to fade,
Colours appear, soft and tender,
Painting the sky in hues of hope.

And I, a witness to this daily miracle,
Feel my spirit rise with the light,
Grateful for the beauty that the dawn brings—
For the simple joy of being alive.

A Tranquil Lunch by the Canal

On my lunch break, I slip away,
leaving behind the hum of screens and calls.
I ride my bike beside the quiet canal,
searching for a moment just for me.

The water flows softly, a gentle reminder
of the peace that waits beyond my desk.
Each pedal stroke takes me further from the day
and closer to a rhythm that calms my mind.

The willows lean in as if to greet me,
their branches brushing against my thoughts,
whispering stories of those who wandered here
before the rush of deadlines took their place.

No need for chatter, just the sound of wheels
and the soft rustle of leaves in the breeze.
As I glide along this familiar path,
I find solace in the stillness,
a brief escape where I can breathe
and reconnect with the woman
behind the work.

In this lunch hour, I hold close the moment
where the demands of work fade away,
and I can simply be,
caught between the past
and my own unfolding story.

Buddy

Upon a gentle purr, the cat awakens,
Startled, it leaps, effortlessly over the wall.
Amongst tall grass and thorny bushes,
It disappears, becoming one with the undergrowth.

A sound, a scent, captures his attention,
The cat's tail sways, a metronome in the breeze.
Eyes focused, steady, locked onto his prey,
Patiently, he waits, poised to strike.

Crouched low, hindquarters ready to pounce,
The cat's paws find firm ground,
Eyes narrow, back arches with tension,
His tail raised high, a flag of determination.

Silently, the cat moves forward,
Each step measured, deliberate.
Muscles coiled, ready to unleash power,
It creeps closer, a predator in the night.

Prey exposed, vulnerable in the moonlight,
Hind legs prepare for the final leap.
In one swift motion, the cat captures his prize,
Playfully tossing it, relishing the thrill.

Tired of the game, the cat releases his plaything,
The victim lies motionless, defeated.
With a quick snap, the cat ends his existence,
A final blow, an act of feline supremacy.

Through the gate, the cat struts with pride,
His tail aloft, a symbol of triumph.
With regal grace, he presents his trophy,
A gift for the lady of the house.

A smile graces her face,
She strokes the cat's head,
Acknowledging his prowess, his skill.
A demanding meow, a request for reward,
A treat for the victorious conqueror.

Curled up in a cosy ball,
Tail and paws entwined,
Whiskers twitching in contentment,
The cat succumbs to sleep.
Yet in slumber, he remains ever alert,
Senses sharp, attuned to every sound.

Gooseberries

You give me jars of gooseberry jam,
hairy amber orbs, bittersweet treasures,
capturing the sun's warmth in each spoonful.
Gooseberries, ripe and ready for picking
when the elderflowers bloom in the hedges,
versatile enough to weave into memories.

Among the pickers, we keep our distance,
nestled in spiny thickets on a summer's day,
from dawn to dusk, weary yet content,
our laughter mingling with the rustle of leaves,
as legend has it, we gather once a year.

Ah, sweet memories are conjured—
gooseberry puddings, tangy preserves,
cold delights savoured, each bite a reminder
of sun-drenched afternoons,
when time melts like the last spoonful of jam,
and love is tasted in every bittersweet morsel.

Moyteoge Head

Standing at the edge of Moyteoge Head,
I breathe in salty air.
The sea stretches endlessly,
inviting me into its depths.

The old coastguard house nearby,
a relic of time, whispers
through the wind tugging at my jacket,
reminding me of lives who once watched
over these waters.

To my left, Croaghaun rises,
its rugged silhouette cloaked in mist,
while Slievemore looms ahead,
a silent guardian of this wild landscape.

I trek southeast, where the Minaun Cliffs
jaggedly greet the crashing waves.
Each step a reminder of raw beauty,
the power of nature unfurling before me.

The wind howls, a fierce companion,
carrying echoes from the sea.
Each gust urging me to venture closer,
to peer into the abyss below.

Three hundred and fifty meters of sheer drop—
my heart quickens as I navigate the edge.
The thrill of the unknown ignites my spirit,
fuelling my desire to explore.

I pause, capturing this moment.
The camera clicks, freezing the view,
but the memory will linger long after,
etched in my mind like the cliffs.

The river flows through steep gulleys,
leading me to Bunowna's ruins,
where shadows of the past stretch long,
and history breathes in the quiet stillness.

I wander past Boycott's estate,
where the air hangs heavy with stories.
The penal altar stands solemn,
a testament to time and sacrifice.

At Keem, the coastguard station comes
into view,
its whitewashed walls bright against
fading light.
I sit, the bay sprawling before me,
reflecting on the day, the journey,
the wildness around me.

As twilight descends, my spirit lifts—
the magic of cliffs and ocean weaving
through me.
This hike, a connection to the earth,
a reminder of where I belong,
among the wild and free.

In the Still of Night

In the hush of midnight,
when the world holds its breath,
two souls drift together,
like leaves on a gentle stream.

Not searching for love,
discovering it in unexpected places,
where stars gather and whisper,
and the moon watches with a knowing gaze.

They wander through the shadows,
unravelling the threads of their stories,
each shared laugh a brushstroke,
painting a scene rich with light.

In the dance of night,
they find the beauty of belonging,
the warmth of a shared glance,
the magic woven in the silence
between words.

And when dawn breaks,
golden light spilling over the horizon,
they carry the glow of their meeting,
a spark igniting the day ahead.

In that stillness, they understand:
love is not always a grand entrance,
often a quiet invitation
to simply be together,
beneath the vast, starry sky.

Aunty May

I mark the years in roses,
Deep and red.
As the clocks go back,
And wintertime begins.
I carve your face in the shadows,
I hear your voice in the wind.

Memories engulf me,
of late-night chats,
And endless cups of tea.
Handwritten letters with gifts,
of note paper and chocolate.

Stories that filled me with laughter,
Now bring tears in the October rain.
Shooting stars, red robins,
And white feathers softly fall.

I feel your touch on my shoulder,
When trodden by life's struggles.
Death's soothing finger
Muffles sorrow.

I stand in the graveyard by your headstone,
Roses in my hands.
I pray for your soul, as you lie,
next to your beloved husband.
Memories never leave me,
Making me feel better.
A heart to heart like old times.
I wait for your response,
Alas, no reply.

I make the sign of the cross,
Blow a kiss and say goodbye.

She Says

You say you have no family.
People think you're stupid.
Loneliness is your constant companion.

Why?
Because you're old and frail with grey hair.

You love books; every cell of your being tells us.
You read them from cover to cover.
You are surrounded by photographs
Of your favourite people.

You wear long cardigans and colourful scarves,
Walking slowly, taking your time.
You watch television, anything and everything.
Sometimes, it brings you down.

You say your family has no time.
No one understands you or sees you.
You're all alone.

You feel you have so much to offer,
Emotionally and physically,
No one wants to know.

You say no one would notice,
If you were not around.
No one would cry at your funeral.
And if they did, they would be fake tears,
So, they better not bother,
Showing up at all.

You say it would be nice to have a family.
When told you do,
You refuse to believe it.

You say it would be nice to be wanted,
Accepted, needed. I say,
'You are.'

Corned Beef and Cabbage

I watched her at the sink,
cutting cabbage,
the knife flashing like a silver thread
in the golden sun.

Leaves fell like soft murmurs
into a basin of salty water—
a ritual passed down
through generations.

On the concrete step,
she sat with her cup of tea,
steam curling,
mingling with the scent
of something simmering on the stove.

A lid held the warmth,
the promise of comfort.

She smiled,
lifting the perfect corned beef,
its tender form resting—
a moment of stillness
in the bustle.

Now, as I unwrap the cling film,
preparing plates of mashed potatoes,
corned beef, and cabbage,
I think of how we shift,
the roles we play,
the quiet longing,
the joy of returning smiles,
the comfort found in shared meals,
in the simple act of gathering—
where love, unseen, simmers
beneath the fabric of the everyday.

Sunrise

Vivid morning sunrise paints gold
Across the sky,
Then spreads its warming tendrils,
To stir the slumbering land.

Soft, a pink fluffy veil
Stills the torment of our minds,
As slowly parting rays reveal
A vibrant countryside.

Frantic, the dawn chorus,
A sonata of birdsong,
Defending territory.
Protecting chicks in verdant boughs.

Sweet the birdsong,
Calling across the fields,
As we rise from our beds
To nature's sweet reveille.

Saint Brigid's Day

On Saint Brigid's Day, my daughter arrived,
with a head of auburn hair,
bright against the white sheets,
a small miracle, fragile and new,
as the morning light spilled softly through
the window.

In those early weeks, we faced a battle;
she struggled to gain strength,
losing weight as if the world felt too heavy,
and she stayed in the hospital, a tiny fighter.

Each day was a test of patience and hope;
the beeping machines, the quiet whispers,
waiting for signs of her energy,
holding my breath with each small gain.

In her fragile beginnings, I saw a spark,
a determination that glimmered in her eyes,
like the first light of dawn breaking through,
promising warmth after a long, cold night.

As she grew stronger, I felt the weight lift,
her laughter filling our home,
her auburn hair catching the sun,
a reminder of the life that flourished within.

Brigid's warmth surrounds her still,
a guiding light in every step she takes.
And I look back on that day,
filled with gratitude for the strength we found,
the promise of a life lived with purpose,
where love reaches out to touch every heart.

PART TWO

First Love

In the quiet of winter's embrace, she sits,
A solitary figure wrapped in the warmth
of memory,
Her heart, a tapestry woven with threads
of the past,
Where her first love danced like sunlight
through leaves.

She closes her eyes, and there he is—a smile,
A glimmering light that lit her days like dawn,
His touch, a whisper of spring on her skin,
And in the depths of her heart,
the coals of affection glow.

The crackling fire hums a familiar tune,
A refuge from the cold breath of winter,
She reaches for a well-worn book,
Pages filled with echoes of love's
tender journey,
Diving deep into the moments that time
cannot steal.

Many hearts have cherished her
through the years,
Some fleeting, some true,
yet none could rival
the depth of her first love,
who beheld her spirit,
who held her close,
with grace through the seasons,
And loved the lines
that time etched on her face.

Gazing upward, she whispers to the stars,
Wondering where love's path has wandered,
Yet in the quiet chambers of her heart,
Her first love lingers, a gentle ghost,
A flame that flickers softly, from beyond the veil of time.

My Guiding Light

In the damp earth of Mulhuddart,
where you rest,
I struggle to picture you.
Instead, I see you on that old garden bench,
steady hands packing tobacco in your pipe,
the calmness in your face,
a cherished memory.

I think of lazy afternoons in Skerries,
your smile bright against the blue sky,
radiating joy as you shared stories,
making each moment feel like treasure,
a gift wrapped in laughter and love.

I remember the roof in Lourdes,
where I brought you, just before the end,
the city sprawling below, quiet and still,
sipping tea, sharing thoughts,
finding solace in the soft breeze.

I won't think of you buried in clay,
because autumn whispers,
and I'm finding my way.

As I walk beside the canal, memories guide me,
your spirit shining bright, a gentle light,
reminding me to embrace the path ahead.

Is it a Lie?

Is it a lie when we fail to ask
the questions that need to be posed?
When silence settles like a mask,
and truth remains undisclosed?

Is it a lie when words fall short,
and omissions breed deceit?
When what we hide becomes a sport,
and honesty feels incomplete?

Or is it only when we know
the answer that we cannot face,
that truth is veiled, and we must show
the lie we cannot trace.

For in the end, a lie is this:
a truth that we refuse to see,
a painful, unwelcome abyss
that we cannot bear to be.

Why Did You Not Call?

I stood by the shore, gazing at the sea,
In search of solace, of what could be.
The waves whispered secrets, tales untold,
As I sought the answers
that my heart longed to hold.

Why did you not reach out when darkness fell,
When shadows danced, casting their spell?
Could you not hear my plea, my silent plea,
As I wondered why you chose to flee.

Why did you not call, and share your dreams,
To bridge the distance, to sew the seams?
Did the winds of change carry you away,
Leaving me adrift, lost in dismay?

Moments slipped through my fingers,
fleeting and fast,
As I pondered the void,
the moments that passed.
Was it fear that drove you,
or doubt's heavy weight?
Did you lose your way, in the depths of fate?

Though your call never came, my spirit remained,
I learned to stand firm, amidst the pain.
So, I release the questions, set them free,
For the answers no longer define me.

Between Us

In the quiet places
where shadows rest,
I reach for the warmth
of your hand beside mine.

Once we wandered
through fields of sun;
now there is the distance
of a river between us.
Your laughter lingers
like a song in the breeze.
The words we left unspoken
drift like leaves in the wind.

Where did we lose our way?
In the garden of memories,
weeds grew tall
and choked the blooms.

Do you see me through
the space we've made?
Can you feel the longing
that time cannot erase?

The moments we held close
are tangled in the thorns,
a fragile thread pulled tight
beneath the weight of silence.

Yet in the quiet hours,
when the day meets the night,
I hum the melody
of our once joyful song.

For even in silence,
there is a flicker of light,
a hope that one day
we will find our way back.

Not lost, just wandering
on different paths;
I hold onto the belief
that time will bring us near.

So, I send my heart
like a bird in flight,
hoping you will hear
the whispers of my love.

In the Stillness of This Hour

In the stillness of this hour,
When slumber wraps the world,
Darkness softens the flickering lights.
Memories drift like whispers,
Entering my mind as the earth turns,
Another day unfolding gently.

Let me guide you back,
To that first light,
Where the sun rose with promise,
Where moments sparkled with youth,
And hope danced in every song.

I played in the streets,
My laughter weaving through the air,
Dancing beneath ancient trees,
Cloaked in costumes of vibrant rags,
And dreams painted in shadows.

Those days stretched wide before me,
Untouched by the weight of time;
Summer's warmth faded,
The years caught up,
The sun whispered its farewell.

In this hour, I feel time's steady march.
Winter arrives, shedding its weary leaves.
Daylight retreats, surrendering
To the lengthening night,
As the world's glow slips into shadows,
Untangling the threads of memory.

Now, in this moment,
I choose patience and kindness,
Grateful for each day that graces my path.
In this fleeting hour,
Contentment sings softly,
For here, in the embrace of now,
This place is home.

An Unanchored Reality

I envision you as you lie in your bed,
Tugging at blankets, seeking warmth.
Your reality, bleak, dark, and unstable,
As time shifts, altering all that you know.

Your home, a dungeon, a suffocating cell,
Your bedroom, a cage where shadows linger.
Your body, no longer a vision of grace,
A feeble skeleton, a weary form.

Your vision distorted as you strain to see.
It's November now; the chill bites at you.
The cold air nips at your cheeks, nose, and lips,
You retreat deeper into your pillow's embrace.

Your children, long gone,
Your husband now passed.
And everyone you once cherished,
Too busy to look back, too distant to care.

Each hour drags on, the same as the last,
Days blend into weeks, the moments fade.
Months and years slip into oblivion's flow,
Leaving you adrift, with nowhere to go.

Where have the voices, the laughter, all gone?
The patter of little feet, the warmth of a song?
The aromas of homemade bread,
sweet and inviting?

Just another day of silence,
Of emptiness, loneliness.
A reality unanchored, a life in suspense.

The Ageless Warrior

Ninety-four years young, I've got stories to tell,
and a sense of humour that's alive and well.
I may have some wrinkles and a few
creaky bones,
I'll still crack a joke that'll shake your
funny zones.

Life's thrown me curveballs,
some unexpected twists,
I've learned to laugh through it all,
with a playful twist.
They say laughter is the best medicine;
it's true,
So, I've been stockpiling jokes, just for you.

I may not be able to run a marathon race,
but my wit and humour will keep up the pace.
I've got punchlines for days and
one-liners galore,
Making people chuckle is what I adore.

I'll bring the humour, the laughter,
and the cheer,
Life's too short to take things too seriously,
my dear.
So, let's share a giggle and have a good time;
With a joke or two, we'll make the world shine.

In the end, laughter is the key
to being stronger, more determined,
and living blissfully.

Christmas Eve

As the day ends, with the smell of mulled wine,
Of falling snow, white trees, rich sweet chestnut air,
Under the Christmas tree, gifts wrapped in bows of gold,
I imagine similar days that have long passed.
I push my hair from my face and stop to stare,
Riveted by a bright, unstoppable woman—
A pink upturning mouth.

Once again, it is time to come together
In this house, a warm place of reflection
Where, for all time, I remain.
Now, honestly, in the autumn of my life,
I know that I have looked my last at youth.
And even more: each year, I am more fulfilled.

Through my window, the solstice moon,
The last full moon of December, drifts away.
The table is laid with gold cutlery
and red napkins.
Wine glasses reflect the flashing lights.
I sit for a moment and reflect: how lucky I am.

A Christmas Prayer

In the hush of Christmas morn,
I stepped through the door,
A church adorned in festive grace,
Memories in its core.

I entered with a solemn heart,
Under a sacred dome,
Drawn to candles' gentle light,
In this holy home.

Under Our Lady's watchful gaze,
In holders crimson bright,
I lit a quintet of flickering flames,
In the morning's light.

Down the aisle, I walked alone,
In echoes of the past,
Where once my father's hand I held
On my wedding day.

The same path trod behind his coffin,
Bagpipes in the air,
Each step a memory,
Each glance a silent prayer.

The church in Christmas attire,
A tree touching the sky,
A crib of beauty, scene of birth,
Where hope cradled lies.
To my left, a shrine stood still,
To Pope John Paul II of bygone years.

In a corner, quiet and unseen,
I found a place to stand,
While 'Silent Night' in chorus rose,
A gentle, soothing sound.

Tears traced paths on cheeks so worn,
In sorrow's quiet morning.
A prayer whispered for mending bonds,
For love's rekindling light.

'Dear God,' I murmured, heart so torn,
'Guide me on this way,
To heal a rift within my kin,
This Christmas Day.'

In the stillness of that sacred space,
With faith's enduring art,
I sought the strength to bridge divides
And mend a fractured heart.

Mother's Day 2022

In the hospital room, cold and bright,
on this Mother's Day, she sits alone,
watching the world through a window,
missing the touch of a loved one.
Gifts rest by the door, tokens of love,
but silence fills the room, heavy and still.

Three years have passed,
three years since everything changed,
and now another wave rolls in,
keeping families apart;
no visits allowed, just the quiet hum
of machines, distance wrapping around her
like a thick coat, blocking out the warmth
that used to fill these walls.

Her body, tired and worn, carries the weight
of unspoken fears, as March kicks up its chill;
the virus returning like a spectre,
spreading shadows through the halls,
searching for the vulnerable,
for those who need the sun's embrace.

April arrives, and the world outside blooms,
a sky so blue it feels like a promise,
but no gentle kisses touch her cheeks,
no arms to hold her; just longing,
a hunger for connection, for the simple
joy of presence, of laughter shared.

In this solitude, she finds her strength,
holding on to hope, even as she sacrifices
the comfort of companionship.
Yet her heart aches still, yearning
for a hand to hold,
a bittersweet reminder of love,
this Mother's Day, where absence
is felt as profoundly as presence.

Baking with My Mother

In the soft morning mist,
I remember standing in the kitchen
with my mother,
watching her sift six ounces
of self-raising flour
into an old mixing bowl,
its cane pattern
telling stories of its own.

Her hands, aged and skilled,
held a well-worn wooden spoon
as she stirred the ingredients
with care.
I loved how her floral dress
swayed around her knees,
and her silver hair
shimmered with the light of the past.

With a steady rhythm,
she mixed caster sugar,
butter, and eggs,
turning them into a smooth batter.

I waited eagerly
as she scooped the mixture
into paper cases,
each dollop a promise
of something delicious.

The sweet scent filled the air,
and I could hardly contain my excitement.
She smiled at me, warm and inviting,
handing me the wooden spoon,
encouraging me to taste.

On the top shelf,
a tray of cakes awaited,
ready to transform in the oven.
I could hardly wait to see
the magic happen
as the dollops of cream
turned golden.

Gently, she moved the hot cakes
to a wire rack to cool,
stirring strawberry jam
to soften it for spreading.

Then, with little hands of my own,
I joined in,
sprinkling coconut flakes over the cakes,
adding my touch to our creations.

In those simple moments,
we were weaving memories—
precious treasures of laughter,
love, and the sweet joy
of baking side by side
with my mother.

The Dance

In the soft glow of evening,
he watched her, a vision—
eyes like the summer sky,
dressed in crisp white,
while he stood, draped in royal blue,
a tailored jacket,
whispering elegance.

The music wrapped around them,
a gentle breeze in the crowded room,
and he, perched on a bar stool,
was captivated by the way her long hair
caught the light,
gold drop earrings swaying,
tiny stars dangling in the air.

She moved with the grace of wildflowers,
her laughter a spark
as she glided across the floor,
each step a quiet promise,
drawing him into her orbit.

The room glowed amber,
as if the sun had melded into night,
and in her pearl-blue eyes,
he found a universe—
a silent invitation to dance.
With a heart that thudded like a drum,
he took her hand,
lifting her effortlessly—
two souls suspended in time,
lost in the rhythm,
while the world dissolved,
and only the dance remained.

Framed by Grief

On a winding country road,
the white-washed house aglow with candles,
a family gathers for a final farewell.

In the cool of a summer's evening,
a father, a husband, a brother, a grandfather,
beloved and cherished, lies in repose.

Standing two meters apart,
the mourners offer their condolences,
amid the sweet perfume of summer blooms,
whispering memories of a life well-lived.

In the shadow of the pandemic,
grief deepens, sorrow feels inconsolable.
Masked faces hide our expressions,
sanitised hands offer little comfort.

As the Rosary is recited,
the priest places beads in a loved one's hands,
and the cool evening air washes over us.

Bales of hay stand in line,
silent sentinels framed by grief.
Compressed and bound by wire,
they bear witness to the weight of loss.

Yet even in that moment of darkness,
beauty can still be found,
the strength of the human spirit,
and the enduring power of love.

The Ravages of War

In the war-torn land,
children's laughter has long been silenced,
Replaced by the thunderous echoes of conflict.
Why must the innocent pay the heaviest toll
in the theatre of war?

Families, once whole, now lie fractured,
Shattered by violence that has become
their relentless companion.
Why do the shadows of fear
cast their pall over these young lives,
Stealing away their sense of security?

In the rubble-strewn streets,
little footsteps tread cautiously,
Navigating a landscape marred by destruction.
Why are playgrounds replaced
by the remnants of buildings,
Shattered dreams echoing in every
broken brick?

The children's eyes hold the harsh reality
of a world they never chose.
Why must their innocence be tainted
by the atrocities unleashed by adults?

Schools, once vibrant hubs of learning,
Now stand as hollow shells,
Echoing the absence of education and hope.
Why are pencils replaced by the sounds
of gunfire and the cries of the displaced?

Hunger gnaws at the stomachs of these
young souls,
Malnutrition leaves its cruel mark on their
fragile bodies.
Why does the basic right to nourishment
become a casualty of war?

Amidst the chaos,
the haunting wails of grieving parents
pierce the air,
Mourning children lost
to the indiscriminate brutality of conflict.
Why does the world silently bear witness
to sorrowful lullabies sung over tiny graves.

The war's scars extend far beyond
visible wounds,
Etching themselves into the psyches of
young survivors.
Why must the trauma of conflict
become a lifelong companion,
Stealing away their chance for
a normal childhood?

In the tragic narrative of war,
the resilience of children flickers
like a dim flame,
refusing to be extinguished.
Why does the world turn a blind eye
to the stark reality that war leaves in its wake?
Especially for those who bear its weight
most heavily.

Tides of Emotion

In the vast ocean of my soul,
feelings rise and fall.
Waves crash against the shores of my heart,
saltwater kisses my skin,
reminding me of storms that once raged.

Like the sea, my emotions ebb and flow,
from gentle swells whispering secrets
to tumultuous tides that pull me under.
I ride these waves fearlessly,
finding solace in the calm spaces between,
where the light dances on the surface.

Each crest a lesson, each trough a chance to
learn resilience, fierce and unyielding;
refusing to be trapped in dark waters
that threaten to swallow me whole.

In the depths, my feelings find release,
currents that whisper peace into my chaos.
Through the waves of my heart,
I chart my course, embracing the journey,
no matter what happens,
knowing the tide always turns.

PART THREE

Shadows in the Dusk

My father drove that mighty truck,
a solid figure at the wheel,
working through shifts and gears,
his hands rough from toil,
sweat glistening like dew on grass.

The engine strained on winding roads,
bearing delectable treasures,
Gateaux cakes snugly packed—
each delivery a feast,
a taste of joy upon the tongue.

Sometimes, he would take me along,
the bond between us thick as night,
proudly introducing me at each stop,
shopkeepers smiling, offering brown bags,
tiny tokens of affection.

As twilight settled in,
under the soft glow of streetlamps,
we sang songs that filled the air,
our voices a mixture of laughter and joy.

With each mile, our spirits soared,
chasing dreams like shadows in the dusk.
Fatigue draped over him,
yet he bore it like a cloak,
never yielding to the weight.

He would tuck me in the warm truck seat—
a gentle kiss upon my cheek,
as I closed my eyes,
surrendering to sleep.

Oh, my beloved father,
you have journeyed on, leaving me here,
yet your legacy endures,
carved deep within my soul.

With each passing day,
I feel your guiding hand,
a beacon shining bright,
an everlasting flame,
lighting my way through the dusk.

Manipulation of the Heart

In Life's intricate fabric, he appeared.
With hair, a whisper of the years,
His eyes, like secrets, deeply stirred,
A bouquet, soft, his charm endears.

She met him, tentative yet bright,
Unknowing of the threads he spun,
A master of the veiled pleasure,
In warmth, his deceit begun.

He spoke of struggles, love's sweet thorns,
Each word, a brushstroke, fine and rare,
A portrait drawn of sorrows worn,
A dance of lies, beyond compare.

As Time unfurled its quiet truth,
Revealing hints that could not stay,
She learned the lessons, soft yet clear,
In betrayal's whisper, trust gave way.

One treads with care in emotion's hall,
For beneath soft words, shadows creep,
In love's faint echo, hearts may fall,
A gentle manipulation, where trust is lost.

The Unveiled Woman

Upon the stage she stands, in exquisite pain,
Her story etched upon her skin with
crimson stain.
No longer bound by the veil of shame,
She stands revealed; a woman unchained.

Her bareness speaks a truth none can quell,
For in her unveiled beauty, she excels.
She stands alone, yet firm in resolve,
Her courage shows as she refuses to dissolve.

The world gazes upon her in awe and wonder,
Her nakedness does not hold her back.
For in her truth, she finds her greatest power,
And in her strength,
she stands tall like a tower.

Let her be an inspiration to us all,
So, we may find the courage to break captivity,
And stand as she does, bare, beautiful,
and true,
For in vulnerability lies our greatest virtue.

Butterfly

Butterfly, I was there,
As you laid your egg on a leaf.
When your light went on,
The whole world became brighter.

I reached out and touched you.
You fluttered beneath my fingertips.
In that moment as the wind blew,
I knew I would always love you.

I was happy as I sang a lullaby,
Sitting in the warmth of the sun.
Oh, how the lull rocks me,
Chasing dreams into the sea.

I watched you defy the earth's
Rotation against the twilight.
In the faint light at the end of the day,
You flew high into the sky,
You couldn't stay...

Butterfly, how the coldness burns-
The blood that pulses under my skin.
As I touch you, only to find that,
My pride ignited right through you,
And your light has gone out.
Butterfly, I am lost.

Bumblebee

You watched me grow, Mom.
There were milestones I missed along
the way—
things I could not accomplish:
the goals not scored,
the Medals not won.

The steps my feet never took,
the Words my lips never spoke.
In my wide Eyes, you saw no fear,
because you were always near.

Often tired, fragile, and weak,
you were my Strength.
You held me tight,
long into the darkness of the night.

You saw my Tears and wiped them dry,
wrapping me in your Loving arms.
Your Heart was heavy for my trials,
you wore it well,
gracing me with Treasured smiles.

I always knew, I was enough for you, Mom,
even on the Toughest of days.
Your Love never faltered,
your Devotion never wavered.

You thanked God every day for giving me to you,
so don't be sad now, for I am running free.
You'll see me on the lavender bush,
I am a beautiful bumblebee.

I Never Left

I never left, my Tullamore Town,
Or my beloved townland of Blue Ball.
On the towpath near the water's edge,
I can hear the din of mallard ducklings.

I never left Boland's Lock,
Even in daylight at a civilised hour,
Where deep purple crocus flowers
bathe after the rain.

I never left; I still watch from Digby Bridge
The sunrise and the sunset,
Like a sudden daffodil in bloom.
Yellowing clouds, the lock chamber,
The backdrop to my reveries, by the dock.

I never left the scent of freshly cut grass,
Or the smell of green algae floating
in the slick,
As I watch the long, delicate dragonfly
Glide serenely and lap up pools of rain.

I never left the music,
The harmony of deep emotion,
To the rhythm of a violin played with a bow:
The melodic sound of rippling waves
makes my heart soar.

I never left; I am with them,
The children in uniform, small and serious.
And the pupils from my old school in
maroon cardigans,
As the crowd sings 'A Woman's Heart'.

I never left my country town,
Nestled in the Slieve Bloom Mountains,
Where quaint little villages step back in time.
The rolling hills still blow me
a breezy smile.

Childhood Memories

In the summer of '76,
we roamed freely, no screens to dim the sun—
only whispers of adventure,
rucksacks crammed with sandwiches,
laughter like fireflies through the trees.

With my brothers, sisters, and our dog, Brownie,
we climbed high, hearts wild with curiosity,
cows grazing, deer standing watch;
in their quiet presence, we learned to linger,
nature's gentle embrace cradling our play.

We scaled trees, bold and alive,
football and rounders painting our afternoons,
hide and seek stretching time,
swinging from ropes, racing gable walls—
the thrill of the chase echoing in our hearts.

Friends from the neighbourhood filled our days,
walking and cycling, chasing horizons,
days in Phoenix Park, wandering Dublin Zoo—
endless possibilities swirling in the breeze,
each moment a brushstroke on our youth.

Transforming the world into our playground,
cardboard dens became secret hideaways,
laughter spilling like sunlight,
brightening every corner of our lives.

We splashed in puddles,
mud squelching beneath our shoes,
LPs spinning softly, melodies drifting—
dancing freely, our voices rising,
innocence wrapped in the rhythm of those days.

Pancakes made in the muck,
screams mingling with wriggling creatures—
our ritual, 99s from the ice-cream man,
sweet moments melting on eager tongues.

Glass bottles of milk on the doorstep,
each memory a treasure, a light in our hearts;
childhood held close, a world untouched
by shadows,
in that radiant summer of '76.

Echoes of Baravore – The Old Crusher House

The old crusher house, a relic of time's
slow hand.
Labour's sweat and life's breath intertwine,
weaving tales through every stone and lintel,
a narrative carved deep.

In the cradle of a stone wall,
a wagtail brood nestles,
their parents darting back and forth,
tireless in their care,
life's stubborn will amidst the toil.

At dawn, vibrant wagtails flit across the scaffold,
feathers aglow like the first light,
tails flicking in rhythm as they
dance on weathered wood.
Lizards, secretive beneath nature's grip,
once found peace in these stones.
Now, the stir of restoration
has disturbed their home.
They slip between cracks,
leaving whispers of their passage.

Sadie, the faithful collie, sits in the
excavator's seat,
a sentinel in the quiet,
watching as deer and wild goats wander
the hills.
Overhead, buzzards fly through the blue,
seeking solace in the endless expanse.

Lugduff's embrace, the morning's tender kiss,
weaves together rain-soaked days
and the stubborn hiss of toil,
crafting a masterpiece of nature.

The water wheel's pit echoes stories of
storms past,
where fury etched marks on its weathered face.
A stone lintel, dormant for sixteen years,
awakens as stonemasons devote their labour
to the art of revival.

Hot lime, sand, and pebbles blend, joints align,
and the trowel's smooth touch glides;
a dance of past and present.
Mortar wrapped in hessian dries along
Avonbeg's edge,
a moment poised for revelation.

Across generations,
skilled hands push back against time's decay,
singing a chorus of history.
Threads of old and new weave together.

A Miners' Week Beneath Glass Mountain's Veil

Monday morn, with the sun's first ray,
We gather 'neath Muckish Mountain grey.
Silica miners, sturdy and true,
Our working week begins, a journey we pursue.

In tunnels dim, our footsteps resound,
As pickaxes strike the earth's deep ground,
With every swing, a rhythm takes flight.
In unison we toil, our purpose alight.

Tuesday dawns, with weariness in our bones,
Determination fuels our steady tones,
Through winding paths and rocky maze,
We press ahead in the dim-lit haze.

Wednesday whispers of fatigue,
Yet camaraderie uplifts; the spirit's intrigue.
With laughter and stories, we find respite,
Forging bonds stronger in this subterranean site.

Thursday's twilight veils our weary faces,
Yet hope sustains us in these confined spaces.
Silica dust may cling, and muscles ache,
Our hearts beat strong, a resolute quake.

Friday arrives, the end within our sight,
As we delve deeper, perseverance takes flight.
Silent prayers for safety as we navigate,
Seeking the treasures that lie in this
fragile state.

Saturday's sun descends,
casting shadows deep,
Yet we push on, our commitment to keep.
For the men of Glass Mountain, this work's
our creed—
Extracting beauty from darkness with
persistence and speed.

Sunday brings a well-earned rest,
As we emerge from tunnels,
dust on our chest,
For in this week's toil, a story is told,
Of the miners' journey—resolute and bold.

Through triumphs and challenges,
we carry on,
With unwavering spirit, our purpose drawn.
Silica miners, united—
A tale of resilience, forever to be recited.

Edenderry –
Echoes of a Bygone Era

In the quiet streets of Edenderry,
Stories drift like morning mist—
Days when life was simple,
And traditions were everywhere.

For fifty years, the Shoe Company stood,
In the hearts of families, making more than shoes.
It built pride, a legacy of craft,
A bond of hardworking hands.

Textile mills hummed with energy,
The forge roared, metal's heartbeat.
Neighbours, as familiar as the hills,
Worked together, laughing and toiling.

Men with calloused hands and strong spirits
Were the backbone of Edenderry.
From peat bogs to the busy mills,
Their work was the lifeblood of the town.

Bord na Móna shaped the land,
With the scent of damp earth in the air.
Fires warmed the hearths on cold nights,
Where stories were shared.

The market square, full of life,
Was the town's heartbeat.
Merchants showed their goods,
And locals chatted—a lively scene.

Carbury, nearby, added its own touch
To Edenderry's rich tapestry.
Stories and traditions woven together,
Creating a community with deep roots.

The local church stood tall,
Its spire reaching the sky.
Sunday sermons offered comfort,
Guidance for those who sought it.

Founding fathers, strong and brave,
Carved their lives from the land.
They inspired generations to value
Hard work, perseverance, and a sense of place.

Today, Edenderry blends its past with
the present,
Creating memories for its people—
A town that cherishes its roots,
Celebrating its history and identity.

Seamus Heaney – A Decade's Tribute

In fields of words and verses pure,
a poet's legacy shall endure.
Seamus Heaney, wise and free,
a decade gone, yet still with me.

His pen, a spade, unearthed the past,
in lines of beauty, memories cast.
Ten years have passed, his light still gleams,
in rivers of thought, in woven dreams.

Through bog and blade, he found his way,
his words, a bridge to yesterday.
With ink and heart, he forged a trail,
the Master's words will forever prevail.

Year's End to New Beginnings

As I look back on the fading year of 2023,
It was a rugged road, tough as can be.
I saw dreams flicker like candles in the wind,
While hope, so fleeting, was hard to pin.

The night wrapped me in a silence profound;
Even in daylight, comfort was rarely found.
Alone in the darkness, I faced down my fears,
Sweeping away a year's worth of tears.

My tears, they fell, telling stories of grief,
A year of losses beyond belief.
My heart took the brunt of time's
relentless pace;
Each silent moment, an empty space.

Loneliness greeted me at each day's start;
In the quiet, despair played its part.
Sacrifices I made, now whispers in the mist—
Fleeting memories of what I've missed.

Yet, amid the struggle, hope remained,
A quiet belief that happiness could
be regained.

In the shadow of the year now gone,
a faint light—
A hint of dawn after the longest night.

Hope and Greed

In halls of kin where shadows breed,
Greed's poison sown, a toxic seed.
Within this fold, a family's plight.
Injustice thrives, concealed from light.

Elders once revered, now pawns in play,
Coerced and abused, their voices sway.
Beneath the weight of avarice cold,
Families crumble, their tales unfold.

Money's grip, a vice, deadly wound,
Fraying bonds once tightly bound.
Avaricious whispers, secrets unfold,
As control and bullying tales are told.

Yet, in this verse, a plea to find
A way to heal, the heart to bind.
For families torn by greed's cruel art,
May love salvage what's torn apart.

Ripples of Time

As time moves forward, I am reminded
of the ripples that once spread out
across the pond of my youth,
and now, like echoes of a distant shout,
they fade away into the depths
of a memory that I can barely grasp.

For as I age, the waters of life
seem to move at an ever-quickening pace.
And like the ripples that never return
to the place where they first began,
I too must accept that time marches on
and that life is just a fleeting span.

No longer can I hold on to youth,
or cling to what has long since passed,
for every moment that I waste
is one that I can never get back.

And so, I let the ripples fade
into the darkness of the deep,
as I embrace each new day with grace
and let go of the past that I cannot keep.

For in the end, it's not the ripples
that define the life that we have led,
but the way that we have loved and lived,
and the memories we have left behind instead.

Justice

Garda Gibbons walked along the Liffey wall;
standing for a moment on the bridge.
He flipped the pages of his notepad;
another victim, orphaned children,
a mother's life extinguished.

Family members with haunted eyes,
motionless; static; frozen with fear.
The Court Clerk addressed the assembly,
"All rise",
eyes flicked to the corner,
looking for the man they despised.

From the holding cell, the monster stirred,
dark suit, white shirt, and tie.
Handcuffed, sullen, red sunken stare,
head held low, clammy palms,
face twisted with despair.

Garda Gibbons did her proud,
he talked of how she was full of fight.
He told her story as he recollected her
last night,
"She looked pathetic, pitiful", he said.

"Bald patches where he pulled her hair,
her clothes, ripped, torn and tattered.
Finger marks on her neck,
scared, bruised, and battered."
The Jury retired;
in a holding cell, he awaited his fate.
Cold air, condensation, windows blurred,
freedom, independence, slipped away.

The crowd was silent; the jury foreman stood,
the verdict was given; the judge stood up.
"Guilty, take him down",
a scream was heard.

He looked up, then dropped his head
in shame,
the mob chanted, pushed, waved their fists.
He stumbled on grey hard steps,
blood trickled down his face.

He was lifted into the waiting prison van;
doors slammed shut, the engine roared.
Locked, handcuffed in a single cell,
brakes came to a halt.

Doors opened; his eyes struggled to adjust.
Wardens waited, heavy keys, metal gates.

Cold breeze, cold shower, prison clothes,
bed linen, metal cup and plate.

Inmates roared, clapped the bars;
within the prison cell, his fears grew.
Keys turned in the door,
he fell to the ground.

Silent tears flowed down his tormented face;
he thought of his wife,
lying in the cold earth.
He wished he could take her place.

PART FOUR

Boy Racer

At the crossroads of life, I stand,
With key in hand and a sporty plan,
Heart racing, adrenaline high,
Gonna push it to the limit, flyin' by.

Kickin' the clutch, hear the engine roar,
Feelin' alive, ready to explore,
Leavin' doubts and fears in the dust,
Gonna hit the road, do what I must.

My mind races with ADHD flair,
But the speed gives me a sense of air,
A freedom from the chains that bind,
As I leave my worries far behind.

Sometimes fear creeps in my mind,
Risking it all, I'm not blind,
But my ride's my trusty steed,
Safely carryin' me through each need.

Navigatin' life's twists and turns,
My ride's my guide, my passion burns,
Embracin' the rush and the thrill,
Of clipping ditches with a skillful will.

So I thank my sporty ride and all it brings,
As I journey on with the wind in my wings,
With heart wide open and spirit free,
This boy racer's life is the life for me.

Ballad of McGrath's Army

In Listowel's Castle, rebellion brewed,
McGrath's Army silently arrived.
Word spread like wildfire through the Town,
Poets and writers ready to astound.

In Writers' Week's name, they took their place,
United by a shared passion.
Born from dreams of Keane and MacMahon,
To celebrate the power of the POEM.

With steadfast purpose, they marched ahead,
To honour Listowel's literary thread.
The Castle's steps, a symbol strong,
Bearing witness as they righted the wrong.

On that summer day, fifty souls arose,
Each with words their hearts composed.
With paper-clad verses, they took the stage,
A rebellion of voices, an impassioned outrage.

No longer bound by convention's hold,
They sought to create, to be bold.
Straw hats adorned heads in the blazing sun,
A unified front, their battle had begun.

McGrath's Army, an army of words,
Their voices like thunder, sharp as swords.
Defiant souls, breaking through the norm,
Leaving an indelible mark, a literary storm.

In Listowel's rebellion, the spirit thrived,
The reasons it started, the founders' drive.
FIFTY years of success, a testament true,
To the resilience of the writers' crew.

So let the tale of McGrath's Army resound,
In Listowel's history, forever renowned.
A rebellion of art, of stories untold,
Writers' Week's spirit, forever bold.

Macken Street

Oblivious to your plight,
I watched my train come into sight.
I settled into a window seat,
Closed my eyes to dream.

I saw you as I crossed
The Samuel Beckett Bridge.
My eyes drawn to your silhouette,
Tall and thin, in dark clothes, a beard.

You booked the penthouse suite,
Barricaded the door.
You stopped the builders.
They didn't lift a brick.

Emergency services stood by;
If you jumped, you would die.
I walked up the steps to start my day,
Sat at my desk, confused and lost.

The blinds drawn tight, blocking our view.
One distraction, and you could fall.
As the day wore on,
I couldn't stop thinking of you.

When lunchtime came, I could take no more,
I grabbed my bag and headed for the door.
You wore a jacket to keep warm,
Communicating with two men in uniform.

By 3 PM, I climbed the back stairs,
Peeking through the blinds.
Nine hours of holding on tight,
I prayed you would be all right.

You came down unharmed.
In my world, all was well.
I hoped you would find help,
To overcome your hell.

Captured in a Digital Age

In a digital age, we ceaselessly roam,
In search of connections, we call it home.
On screens, we curate our lives, day by day,
A modern obsession, we cannot delay.

The selfie, a tribute to the self we display,
On Instagram grids, in a colourful array.
I see you, dear reader, through filters and frames,
In pixels and captions we play social games.

Do we wonder, as we wander online,
If these captured moments are truly divine?
In the quest for connection, do we lose our way,
In this digital age, where we live night and day?

So, let us be mindful, as we post and share,
Of the life beyond screens, of moments so rare.
In this modern era, there's so much to be seen,
And life's truest beauty awaits beyond the screen.

The Road Between Us

Even though it was May
and the sun shone bright,
I didn't buy you an ice cream.
I didn't see your smiling face
or take you in my arms.

The road between us was closed,
restrictions in place.
I missed your first birthday.
No path opened from me to you.

Was this war?
Was this what it felt like?
Families torn apart,
no time to prepare.
Days, weeks, months
engulfed in bad news—
people died alone,
without a warm hand to hold
or a loved one to say goodbye.

No words of comfort,
no hugs, no handshakes
for grieving families.
Strangers stood in line along the roadside
as the hearse carried them home.

Space and social distance
the new norm—
masked faces, gloved hands—
a world I never wanted for you.

Trees were in spring blossom then,
a celebration of winter's end.
I waited to see you.
Perhaps you were waiting too.

Love,
Nanny

Photographer's Journey at Serenity's Cove

On the peaceful shores of Serenity's Cove,
A solitary man wakes with the first light of day,
His camera held gently in his hands.
With a steady step, he walks to the beach,
Drawn by the beauty of the rising sun.

Silently, he finds his spot on the soft sand,
Becoming part of the landscape,
As the sound of waves fills the air around him.
He waits patiently for the right moment
To appear before his lens.

As the sky begins to wake,
A burst of colour unfolds,
Painting the horizon in gold, pink, and orange.
The man's focused gaze watches the scene,
His camera ready to capture the stunning view.

With each click of the shutter,
He freezes the fleeting beauty of dawn.
The quiet beach becomes his safe place,

A space where he can lose himself
in photography,
Where time seems to pause.

Through his lens, he captures
The play of light and shadow,
The gentle reflections on the water.
Each photo tells its own story,
A record of the solitary journey
He takes each day.

In this calm solitude,
He finds peace and connection.
The beach becomes his inspiration,
Offering a place to show his love
For the natural world.

With every sunrise, he remembers
The vast beauty that exists
Beyond his own thoughts.
As morning unfolds and the sun rises higher,
He reluctantly puts his camera away,
Taking with him the images he has captured,
Memories etched in his mind.

Until tomorrow, he says goodbye
To Serenity's Cove, knowing
The beach will always welcome him back,
Ready to share its secrets once more.

The Bridge

From my office high, I watch the world below;
The Liffey flows gently, its waters soft
and slow.
Above it stands a sight that captures
my gaze—
The Samuel Beckett Bridge, a wonder
in the haze.

I saw it come in, towed carefully through
the bay,
Built piece by piece, changing night into day.
It's shaped like a harp, reaching up to the sky;
A bridge of hope and dreams.

The city spreads beneath, with stories in
each stone—
Of laughter and of heartache,
Of lives we've never known.
The Convention Centre glows, a light against
the dark,
In Docklands, where shadows leave
their mark.

Yet still my heart is pulled
To this bridge so bold and bright,
A symbol of our journey, standing strong in the night.

Samuel Beckett Bridge, you rise with quiet grace,
A sign of our connection in this familiar place.
As footsteps drift like whispers,
And wanderers pass near,
You share a song of promise beneath the sky so clear.

Benbulben

I stood spellbound
As the mountains plateaued,
Majestic Benbulben,
A titan of limestone and shale,
Over three hundred million years ago,
When glaciers blanketed the earth.

I climbed the steep ascent,
Careful over sheer edges,
The wind slapping my face,
Urging retreat.

Scenic views stretched wide,
Towering peaks loomed,
Rugged outlines against the sky,
Each ridge and valley ancient.

Below, rolling hills and fields,
Lush green, swaying in the breeze.
The sky shifted from grey to blue,
Sunlight breaking through,
Casting warmth across the land.

Stone ruins dotted the landscape,
Echoes of those who walked before.
The path ahead wound upward,
Beckoning me to explore.
Trancelike, I stood on Irish soil,
Where W.B. Yeats rests,
Surrounded by history.
At one with the mountains,
The sun warmed my skin,
Filling me with peace.

Nollaig na mBan

In the morning light,
A day just for you.
When the world slows down
To notice what you do.
Dishes stacked like stories,
Laundry in a heap,
You've stitched love into each thread,
Each memory to keep.

Through laughter and tears,
Your quiet strength shines.
You've walked paths of resilience,
Crossed many lines.
Today, let the men take charge in the kitchen.
With laughter and joy,
Let the day be their mission.

No late nights to worry,
No early starts to face.
Let them share tales,
Let them find their own pace.
While you take a moment to breathe,
To celebrate the heart that has given so much.

So, here's to the women,
Both near and far.
Your hearts are the home,
The light in our days.
On this Nollaig na mBan,
We honour who you are,
With love and gratitude
In countless ways.

Bloomsday

In Dublin's streets, on Bloomsday's eve,
Where Joyce's spirit forever weaves.

Oh, James Joyce, the master's name,
Whose pen ignited a literary flame,
He crafted tales, intricate and vast,
In *Ulysses*, his opus unsurpassed.

Bloomsday dawns with reverent might,
A day of homage, an artistic rite,
Through Dublin's lanes, we stroll and roam,
To the places where his characters found home.

In Molly's boudoir, desire ablaze,
In Leopold's heart, the wanderer's gaze,
Through Stephen's thoughts, a seeking mind,
Joyce's tapestry intricately entwined.

We tread the paths of Dublin's past,
In search of echoes that forever last,
In pubs and cafés, we raise a toast,
To the prose that transcends,
delights the most.

Beneath a June sun's gentle kiss,
We find solace in linguistic bliss,
For Bloomsday speaks of human grace,
In the everyday, its sacred space.

The ordinary lives, he did unveil,
In Dublin's streets, his words prevail,
From dawn to dusk, a single day's plight,
Bloomsday unveils the depth of the night.

Through Molly's thoughts, intimacy blooms,
In Leopold's kindness, compassion looms,
Stephen's quest for wisdom untold,
In these characters, our souls enfold.

Oh, James Joyce, your genius complete,
Through plain words, your truth was found,
On Bloomsday, we honour your poetic art,
A pilgrimage to the depths of the human heart.

Twelve Crosses at Ballybraid

On the slope of Ballybraid,
twelve wooden crosses stand,
Reminding us of a troubled past,
Where Cromwell's soldiers left their mark,
And twelve lives were lost.

Here lie Catholics who gathered for Mass,
Their lives taken suddenly, cruelly.
They rest where trees have been cut down,
And their stumps seem to mourn.

Lavender and gorse grow nearby,
A sign of hope amid the sadness.
The dark wooden crosses stand in silence,
Each one a marker for those who fell,
In this sacred place of remembrance.

The wind howls around us,
While silence wraps us gently.
Mountain sheep roam peacefully,
Watching over restless souls.

The living might forget the past,
But we gather here to remember.
In this special place, we honour the lost,
Their sacrifices will not be in vain.

The climb is steep; at each grave,
We find moments of stillness in our hearts.
Ashes may fade, and smoke may rise,
Yet the spirits of the dead linger on.
In this sacred space where we find peace.

Let the living and the dead be connected
In this high place,
Where memories are kept quietly,
Echoing softly, a gentle presence.

In this place of grief, we find our way
Through the shadows of the past,
Honouring those who have fallen,
Whose spirits remain with us always.

In the Darkness of the Night

I was familiar with the night.
I hiked through the rain and fell in the rain.
I walked in darkness,
with just a headlight.

I looked down steep mountain ranges,
passed the sika deer; our eyes met,
I lowered my gaze,
unable to remain.

I stood still, watching the hind retreat,
when far away, a guttural cry
rolled over the mountain from a stag,
not to call me back, nor say goodbye.

And further still, at an unearthly height,
one luminous moon against the sky
declared a fall on slippery ground,
neither wrong nor right.

I was one familiar with the night.

Trapped in an Hourglass

In the crowded room, she stood,
Hidden in the laughter,
Her heart a quiet whisper, lost in the noise.
Trapped in an hourglass,
Surrounded by warmth,
Yet feeling cold.

The air felt thick,
As she stayed still, like a lonely tree.
Life swirled around her, lively and bright,
Yet she felt tied down,
Like a leaf caught in the wind.

An empty shell among smiling faces,
Her pain hidden behind a gentle smile,
An unseen weight, a shadow in the light.
The ground shook beneath happy footsteps,
And still, she stood, a quiet observer.

Longing for a glance from someone nearby,
Hoping to close the gap between them.
For now, the hourglass held her back,

Waiting for a change,
To lift the glass and find her way home,
Where love can grow freely,
And hearts reconnect under the open sky.

About the Author

Sandra Behan is an Irish poet whose work is rooted in the landscapes and traditions of her homeland. Inspired by Ireland's rugged beauty, her lyrical performances captivate audiences at events like 100 Lights and Glenmalure Heritage Week.

Her debut poetry collection, *Unveiled*, invites readers to explore emotional depths through warm recollections of childhood and family, alongside reflections on world events and personal relationships, all infused with a strong sense of place.

Sandra began her writing journey in Listowel in 2008, participating in her first workshop at the Kerry Writers' Museum with Leo Cullen. She has since become a familiar voice at Listowel

Writers' Week, engaging in events such as the 'Healing Session' at John B. Keane's bar. Her work has been published in *A Page from My Life* ('Mark Twain Bent Pipe'), as well as in the Kerry and Wicklow newspapers and various poetry collections for charity.

She is currently working on her debut novel, 'Daniel'. In addition to her literary pursuits, Sandra is a mother of three and grandmother of three. She is also a member of the Carbury Players drama group, where she made her stage debut in the two-act play *Cash on Delivery*, portraying Dr. Chapman.

www.ingramcontent.com/pod-product-compliance
Lightning Source LLC
Chambersburg PA
CBHW060454080526
44584CB00015B/1430